THE
Archive Photographs
SERIES
AROUND
ABINGDON

The Abbey Gate, c. 1900. This is probably a Monday photograph taken by Abingdon photographer Warland Andrew. The sheep, waiting for market, may have been driven from a neighbouring village and await going to sale in the sheep market, now the Square.

THE
Archive Photographs
SERIES

AROUND
ABINGDON

Compiled by
Nigel Hammond

CHALFORD

First published 1996
Copyright © Nigel Hammond, 1996

The Chalford Publishing Company
St Mary's Mill, Chalford,
Stroud, Gloucestershire, GL6 8NX

ISBN 0 7524 0392 3

Typesetting and origination by
The Chalford Publishing Company
Printed in Great Britain by
Redwood Books, Trowbridge

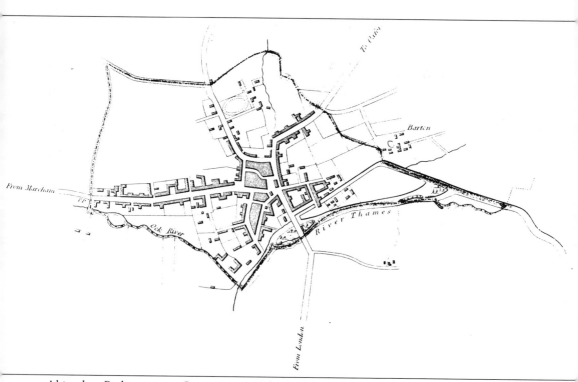

Abingdon Parliamentary Constituency. The last Member of Parliament for the Borough of Abingdon was John Creemer Clarke of Waste Court in Bath Street. He was Liberal in sympathy and first elected in 1874, re-elected in 1880 and continued to represent the Borough until the dissolution of 1885, when it ceased to return a member.

Contents

Foreword

by Sir James Cobban, CBE, TD, DL. Headmaster of Abingdon School 1947-70.

Some fifty years ago, on a dank November day in 1946, I attended an interview in Abingdon which changed my whole life. Through it I became, and still am, an Abingdonian by adoption if not by birth. As Headmaster of Abingdon School it was one of my cardinal tenets that although we might be of far more than local reputation we might never forget our roots. The fact that our sixteenth-century schoolroom in the heart of the town still remained in active use, as part of the municipal building, was a symbolic reminder of our continuing connection.

   As I see it, this anthology will appeal to Abingdonians of all ages. But it will be of special interest to two groups. Firstly, there are those 'oldies' who are so often bemused by all the changes that have taken place in and around Abingdon within the last fifty years. To them, these photographs will be a memoir of the Abingdon they knew and loved.

   Secondly, I am thinking of all those young, and not so young people, in and around the town who may know little of their heritage. In these anarchic days, when all our old-fashioned loyalties came into question, it may help to remind some of them that they are part of a living community, rich in tradition, rich in present interests, rich in hope for the future.

   I have known Nigel Hammond for a long time, as pupil, as colleague, as friend. I know with what meticulous care he will have edited this collection of historic local photographs, I am privileged to commend it to all who share our devotion to the town and its immediate surroundings.

Introduction

Good fortune is unpredictable. It was a summer morning in the mid-1970s that a colleague told me that two sample albums largely of Taunt photographs of Abingdon and around were on sale in his village. I had viewed and purchased the collection before lunch, but for twenty years the photographs remained carefully preserved. One day, I knew, they would be very useful. Consequently, I am pleased this publication of archive photographs enables them now to be seen by a wider audience.

Abingdon-on-Thames is an ancient settlement in recent history focusing on the junction of the River Ock and the Thames and at an important crossing point of the major river towards the direction of London. The great Benedictine Abbey was located just east of the market and close to the river crossing and was a decisive force in overseeing the history of the town until its dissolution in February 1538. The uncertain Borough Ford through the river was replaced by a bridge over the Thames together with an associated causeway across Andersey Island and another bridge at Culham over Swift Ditch by the Guild of the Holy Cross in 1416: this early merchant Guild survives as Christ's Hospital, Abingdon, a major town landowner and charity which is centred on the distinctive sets of almshouses surrounding St Helen's churchyard.

The demise of the Abbey caused some decline in the status of the town and the first charter of 1556 comments that Abingdon 'being the Capital town of Berkshire is in great ruin and decay for want of repairing'. Accordingly Abingdon was constituted a Borough and remained County Town of Berkshire until Reading took over in the 1860s. The County Hall dignified that status, and is perhaps the finest Market Hall in England 'built by Christopher Kempster of Burford and influenced by Christopher Wren his patron' it was completed in 1678. It stands near the site of Abingdon Market Cross, 'a right goodly cross of stone with faire degrees of imagerie' demolished during the Civil War but having been built by the Brethren of the Holy Cross in 1442.

So, it is as a market and commercial centre in Berkshire that Abingdon found its role. Markets took place on Monday and Friday, but George II's Charter (1739) granted a licence also to hold markets on Tuesday, Wednesday, Thursday and Saturday for the buying and selling of all manner of corn and grain.

In addition to the markets, as befitted the County Town, the fairs were among the busiest and noisiest times of the year. The Lent Fair, on the first Monday in Lent, did trade in horses, cattle and sheep. In spring the Bull Fair, alternatively called Lombard Street Fair, traded in horses, cattle, sheep, bulls and cheese. The early June Ock Street Fair traded in cattle and horses but came to be a pleasure fair. In August, St James' Fair had a good business in lambs' wool. The Broad Street Fair in September did swift sales in horses, sheep, fat cattle and cheese, while the Michaelmas Hiring Fair extended the length of Ock Street to the Market Place and was the largest and most important event of the year. The Runaway Fair which followed was to find further employment for labourers and servants who were unhappy with their previous newly-found jobs and had literally 'run away'. The final fair came in December and traded predominantly in cattle, horses and sheep.

But it was the Thames that was of crucial importance to Abingdon. It has turned mill wheels, provided fish and water for irrigation, manufacturing and domestic purposes: it has been a means of trade and communication, a waterway used for centuries for business, pleasure and commerce. The Wilts & Berks Canal opened to Abingdon in 1810 and brought another spur to water transport, enabling cheaper Somerset coal to be brought along the Vale of the White Horse to Abingdon and undercutting Midland coal fetched on the Oxford Canal and expensively transhipped from Hythe Bridge to St Helen's Wharf on the river. But in due course the centres which relied on the canal were linked to the railway. I.K. Brunel's Great Western Railway opened in 1840 from London to Bristol: the intended line from Steventon across the western side of Abingdon to Oxford did not materialise and Abingdon had to wait until 1856 for a branch line from Radley on the Didcot to Oxford line of 1844. This delay, in effect, sealed Abingdon's fate and in due course the substantially expanded town of Reading, more centrally placed in Berkshire, took on the role of County Town.

Commercially, Abingdon was important in woollen cloth manufacture but the business had all but ended by the time of the Civil War. In the eighteenth century spinning and weaving hemp and flax flourished and a sacking, carpet, matting, smock making and clothing manufacture developed. Much malt was traded: even in the mid-nineteenth century there were seven malsters at work in the town: the sole remaining co-related activity is Morland & Co's Brewery in Ock Street and the Maltings in the Vineyard. Small-scale business took place in matting and sacking manufacture, basket making and glove making. The tanning and leather industries gave rise to fellmongers, curriers, leather cutters, boot, shoe and clog makers, harness makers and saddlers. The dirty trades were also important in the town: iron and brass businesses stood beside the whitesmiths who dealt in tin, polished and galvanised iron. Timber trades gave rise to basketmakers, coopers, coachbuilders, cabinetmakers, wheelwrights, carpenters, upholsterers, joiners and printers.

From 1864 came development of the distinctive Victorian suburb set around and to the south of Albert Park: possibly one of the finest Victorian estates outside north Oxford. It was to a site here offered by Christ's Hospital that Abingdon School moved in 1870, as did many of the professional and commercial classes, taking up residence in one or other of the houses designed by local architect Edwin Dolby, who operated from Park Crescent.

More recent developments have seen the rise and fall of the MG car and the Pavlova leather companies. Fitzharry's Manor grounds provided the site for housing employees of the post-war Atomic Energy Research Establishment at Harwell. But in reality, although Abingdon has expanded massively in recent years, matters have come full circle. Abingdon lost its cherished County Town status over a century ago. With more recent reorganisation Abingdon is no longer a Borough, but was transferred with the entirety of north Berkshire to Oxfordshire. Once proudly returning its own Member to Parliament, it now shares a Member with Oxford. Times change with increasing rapidity.

Nigel Hammond
August 1996

One
Abingdon-on-Thames

St Helen's Wharf, c. 1890. A canal barge is tied up in front of the Old Anchor Inn. Another barge unloads at warehouses just beyond the malthouse. The canal was used at this time chiefly for the transport of coal, corn, building and road making materials to Abingdon with only a limited return cargo to the west.

Almshouses in St Helen's churchyard, c. 1890. Brick Alley Almshouses (right) were built in 1718 by Samuel Westbrooke and face across the churchyard to Long Alley Almshouses of 1446. The former Almshouses-over-the-water were demolished in the 1880s: they backed on to the river where steps lead to a wider esplanade on the right. The set of houses west of the Old Anchor Inn on St Helen's wharf were built by Christ's Hospital to replace them in 1884. Nevertheless the Almshouses-over-the-water had a long history and dated from 1424.

St Helen's Wharf, *c.* 1910. A series of pleasure boats is tied up on both sides of the river. The horse in the water beside the malthouse may have pulled the canal barge up to the warehouse beyond, and gives a fair indication that the river may have been shallower at the sides than it is today and appears to be well silted on the Oxfordshire side. The sets of steps were invaluable to bargees, giving access up the wall to the wharf above.

St Helen's Wharf, *c.* 1890. Linking the Thames with the Wilts and Berks Canal wharf is the cast iron bridge made at Acraman's foundry, Bristol, in 1824 which gave access across the River Ock at its junction with the Thames. Buildings from the left include the clothing factory with its high chimney, the Old Anchor Inn, Christ's Hospital, St Helen's church, Brick Alley Almshouses, the malthouse and the County gaol.

St Helen's church from the river, *c.* 1890. The end of Nag's Head Island is on the extreme right; the chimney of the clothing factory, to the right of the spire, was built in 1852 and burnt down in 1944. Barns and warehouses line the river; here coal, malt and iron were traded and transhipped by the Copeland family. On the left is the malthouse and rear of Brick Alley Almshouse. The Copelands had various businesses in the second part of the nineteenth century apart from the main concern behind the malthouse for there were two family butchers' shops and an insurance agency for the Mutual Life Assurance Society.

St Helen's church, c. 1890.
Warehouses have steps leading down
to the river enabling Thames barges
and Wilts & Berks Canal barges to be
unloaded into the premises behind.
These are the warehouses of Ebenezer
Copeland which saw much trade
during the nineteenth century in malt,
coal and iron. The buildings stood
round a substantial yard which had
road access through a narrow exit into
East St Helen Street opposite the
church porch.

Mill Stream, c. 1910. Viewed from
Abingdon Bridge, St Helen's church
dominates this part of the river.
Although narrowly connected to the
main channel of the Thames round the
eastern end of Nag's Head island, the
Mill Stream is largely flowing from the
Abbey Mill in Thames Street whose
double set of millstones it helped turn.

Mill Stream, *c.* 1910. St Helen's church spire is reflected in still water; high walls enclose gardens behind East St Helen Street; the gateways give access for boaters to reach their punts in this high summer and low water-level picture. As one would expect, the Victorians used their gardens to great effect with substantial orchards of laden apple and plum trees in evidence. Fashionable was the habit of building sheds on stilts at the top of the garden for discreet viewing up and down this part of the river, whilst retaining one's own privacy behind high walls, and maintaining the distinct advantage of shade.

Opposite: Rebuilding Abingdon Bridge, 1928. Work is in progress on the then Oxfordshire side of the river. Steps leading down from the road to the towing path along the river bank to Abingdon Lock can be seen at the top. Contractors for this extensive project were James Byrom Ltd. of Bury who presented Christ's Hospital with an album of photographs of the work on its completion; also a substantial bill for the project.

Rebuilding Abingdon Bridge, 1928. Building works are in progress on the main span. Looking across the bridge into Bridge Street, the Nag's Head inn is on the right and the Crown and Thistle in the corner at the top of Bridge Street. This new span and the associated works replaced part of the original Abingdon Bridge built largely for trade purposes in 1416 by the Guild of the Holy Cross, forerunner of Christ's Hospital, Abingdon. Part of the bridge which was replaced is on page 16.

Skating on the Thames. The late Victorian period was well known for hard winters and the river at Abingdon, slower flowing and shallower than today, froze over on several occasions: on one a sheep was roasted on the frozen river opposite the almshouses. Here, four people are on the ice at Abingdon Bridge with bystanders and the Nag's Head Inn above. In the town some call this Burford rather than Abingdon Bridge, the former name being a corruption of Borough Ford which building of the Bridge in 1416 replaced, enabling Abingdon to collar some of the London trade which had crossed the river at Wallingford.

Abingdon Bridge, *c.* 1890. The Nag's Head Inn stands on an island between the Thames and Mill Stream. The downstream portion of the island held the stabling yard. This mediaeval part of the bridge was rebuilt and widened in 1928, the increased size of the navigation arch enabling Salter's steamers from Folly Bridge, in Oxford, to pass downstream with greater ease.

Abingdon Lock, *c.* 1910. Abbot Ordric (1054-66) cut an improved channel for the Thames through Abingdon. The original Abingdon Lock was higher upstream at the entrance to Swift Ditch, formerly the main channel of the river. After 1790 the Abingdon section of the river was re-opened and Swift Ditch fell into disuse.

St Helen's church, *c.* 1894. The spire of St Helen's reflected in part of the river as seen from the only remaining mediaeval portion of Abingdon Bridge to escape rebuilding in 1928. Under the arches of the bridge one can see clearly that it has been widened by a third on the upstream side as increased traffic demanded it be turned from a pack-horse bridge to one capable of conveying a waggon in each direction: this change took place while the bridge formed part of the Abingdon to Dorchester and Henley Turnpike Road.

Two

Around
the Market Place

Market Place, 1857. The obelisk stood near the centre of the market from 1834 until replaced in 1887 by the statue of Queen Victoria presented to Abingdon by Mr Edwin Trendell: at that time the obelisk was re-erected in the Square. The Old Globe Inn on the left of the picture backs on to Stert Street, while Georgian balconies supported by pillars grace the rest of the eastern side of the market. These premises are Wadsworth's furniture warehouse and the Star Tavern. On the corner of the narrows leading into Bridge Street is the gateway into Roysse's School, paid for by the Earl of Abingdon, High Steward of the Borough, about 1811.

The Market Place, c. 1890. The view is looking up Bury Street between the Corn Exchange and Queen's Hotel. Bury Street was the site of several businesses and the new National School which replaced the 1823 school near St Helen's churchyard. The statue of Queen Victoria stood near the centre of the Market in front of the Queen's Hotel and was presented by town tradesmen and former mayor, Edwin Trendell, in 1887 on the occasion of the Golden Jubilee and unveiled by Lord Wantage in June of that year. At the end of the Second World War the statue was removed to the Abbey grounds.

The Queen's Hotel, c. 1864. A Henry Brooks photograph (see page 100) issued possibly as an advertisement card by Morland & Co. Piles of cobbles in front of the building indicate that the setts were being replaced in the Market. This may be an early Brooks' photograph taken before the Queen's was open for business and the front door is firmly shut, windows open as if freshly painted and are quite curtainless.

Market Place, *c.* 1890. A Henry Taunt view of the Market with the London & County Bank, now the National Westminster Bank, on the left, the Corn Exchange built in 1886 to the design of Charles Bell in the centre, and the Queen's Hotel of 1864 facing the County Hall across the cobbled Market. Both Corn Exchange and Queen's Hotel were demolished in the 1960s to make way for the Bury shopping precinct which runs along the line of the old Bury Street to the side of the Corn Exchange site.

County Hall, 1890. This view is framed in the Abbey Gateway. County Hall was completed in 1682; the general plan and elevation may be by Sir Christopher Wren who then left details to the attention of Christopher Kempster of Burford, who was Wren's most trusted builder. The total cost was £2,840. There was a proposal in 1849 to place windows in the lower part and to use this glazed-in portion as a Corn Exchange in what is considered to be one of the finest Stuart civic buildings in England. Fortunately the scheme was shelved and the Corn Exchange built across the Market Place in 1886.

East St Helen Street, 1890. Looking along the street to the rear of County Hall: St Nicolas' church is framed at the end of the street facing on to the Market Place. The Old Bell Inn, now and formerly the King's Head and Bell, served other purposes beside being a beer and drink retailer, and in this case a coal and coke merchant was also in business on the premises. The prosperous-looking houses along the street mark it out as the pre-Victorian residential area for merchants, manufacturers, businessmen and the professional classes.

St Nicolas' church and Abbey Gateway, c. 1900. St Nicolas' church was traditionally a place of worship for the lay people associated with Abingdon Abbey. Being next to the gateway, the eastern part of the church lies within the Abbey precinct and it is still sometimes known as the 'little church in the gate'. Inside is the grand memorial to John and Jane Blacknall who died on the same day in 1625. The Council chamber and court on the right of the gate is on the site of St John's Hospital, whose almsmen were transferred to new premises in the Vineyard in 1800. The gatehouse served as a prison for the Borough until it was converted into the Masonic Room in George IV's time.

Bridge Street, c. 1890. Henry Taunt photographed the street in the early evening after the business of the day had ended. The man waits beside his cart, the Broad Face inn is open at the junction with Thames Street. Next door are the premises of Staniland's cabinet-making and paper-hanging business with a fine chair on the pavement outside. The Crown & Thistle hotel is in the narrows with Berkshire House, a draper and milliner, opposite. Woodbridge's corn merchant building is on he extreme left.

The Abbey Gate, *c.* 1900. Probably a Monday photograph taken by Abingdon photographer Warland Andrew. The sheep, waiting for market, have been driven from a surrounding village and await going to sale in the sheep market, now the Square. The servant accompanying the young girls has been posed to view the flock: they may well have come from Abbey House just visible within the Abbey precinct.

Abingdon Bridge, 1890. A late afternoon conversation piece on that part of the bridge which crosses Mill Stream. The mediaeval bridge of 1416 is extant on the left with the widened portion with pavement opposite. On the left in Bridge Street are the outbuildings of the County Gaol with the roof line of County Hall rising above: on the right stands the Crown & Thistle and St Nicolas' church tower.

93. Abingdon: Abbey Mill & Bridge.   F. F & Cº ..5 ..

Abbey Mill, c. 1900. Thames Street on the left runs into a cul-de-sac by the Abbey buildings. Over Mill Stream the bridge leads on to the island giving access to the mill. This was the site of the hemp and twine works. The Gas Light and Coke Company was also located here to make use of water-carried coal on the river and Wilts & Berks canal: in due course the gas works moved to the railway yard behind Stert Street; the mill has become the Upper Reaches restaurant and hotel. At the Abbey Corn Mill much of the grain from monastic farms in the Vale would have been ground. Just upstream were the Abbey Fulling Mills and after Dissolution of the Abbey there was an attempt to revive the cloth industry here by making sailcloth.

High Street, 1890. Looking east to the Market Place from the junction with West St Helen Street, this late afternoon photograph shows a remarkably uncluttered scene with few vehicles and most of the dozen or so people standing well back in the shade on the right of the street. The Lion Hotel on the left, with entrance arch to the stables at the rear, occupies much of the street: today's Lion is but a shadow of its former self, much of the hotel having been demolished in the late 1920s. It is worth noting how excellently the whole length of the street is paved with stone setts and rougher cobbles to the sides: pavements have a smooth course of York stone.

High Street, c. 1900. Looking west from the Market Place to the junction with West St Helen Street. Buildings on the left are notably unchanged today, but important alterations have taken place on the opposite side of the street. This is the site of the Michaelmas Hiring Fair which extends from the Market Place to the end of Ock Street and at this date might still have seen a hearty throng of carters, shepherds, thatchers and dairy maids seeking employment. The Runaway Fair which followed in High Street and the Market Place a week later was literally for those who had run away from their employment and were seeking a happier position.

West St Helen Street, *c*. 1920. These cottages on the west side of the street near St Helen's church and the clothing factory have given way to modern housing but still give some indication of the conditions in which the working people of Abingdon lived with narrow houses, courtyards, workshops and factories in a haphazard and unhealthy juxtaposition. For instance, the gateway on the left led into a courtyard of squalid dwellings known colloquially as Paradise Square. All these buildings were demolished in the late 1930s.

Thames Street, 1952. Coronation street-party in progress with the deputy mayor, Percy Holmes in attendance, top left. The bridge and entrance into the mill are just visible on the right at the top of the photograph. The Abbey buildings and office of the Friends of Abingdon are on the left of the street.

High Street, 1913. John Roysse re-founded the town grammar school in 1563. It is likely that this picture shows a procession of dignitaries, scholars and townsfolk to mark the 350th Anniversary of the re-foundation of Abingdon School in the Roysse Room. They are in procession to the new buildings erected in 1870 in Albert Park.

Three
Albert Park

Park Road, c. 1900. Some local residents appear posed for the camera, while others may be taking a genuine afternoon walk or bicycle ride. We are looking east along Park Road from a point between St Michael's church on the right and the southern entrance to Albert Park on the left. In the far distance is the recently built lodge to Abingdon School.

St Michael's church, 1890. A rare uninterrupted view of the church from the south-east, for here is now St Michael's Avenue and the housing beside it and each side of the church in Park Road. Interestingly, the main entrance to the church is on the south, for it was primarily to serve the community of dwellers who lived in the narrow courts each side of Ock Street. The church was planned by Revd Nathaniel Dobson, designed by Sir George Gilbert Scott and consecrated on 25 January 1867 by Rt Revd Samuel Wilberforce, Bishop of Oxford.

Albert Park, 1890. This relatively open view to the south shows three Abingdon churches: on the left, Trinity Methodist church (1875), St Helen's church in the centre with the old clothing factory chimney immediately to its right, and St Michael's church (1867) on the right.

St Michael's church, 1890. Looking, here, from the west along Park Road one can see open countryside towards Ock Street. St Michael's Avenue, Bostock Road and the houses along Conduit Road have yet to be built. The Edwardian houses in Park Road now block this view for we are looking across the building plot in due course to be occupied by 30 Park Road. It is good to see the lime trees which now grace Park Road as mere saplings. Until the Spring of 1896 the only access to the church was from the road on the north side. In 1896 the Governor of Christ's Hospital opened a new road, St Michael's Avenue, which gave access to the south porch of the church, described in the Abingdon Parish Magazine for May 1896 as passing through 'an avenue of well-grown Canadian elms'.

Abingdon School, 1890. This is the scene across the gravel at the top of the school drive and is how the school remained until 1901. The small 1880 extension is clearly visible on the right, built during the headship of Revd Edgar Summers (headmaster 1870-1883). The open access to the undercroft playground in the 1870 building below Big School (now the Grundy Library and John Hooke Library) faces on to the gravel. The undercroft was glazed and turned into a dining hall by William Grundy (headmaster 1913-1947) which function it continued to fulfil until 1974.

Abingdon School, 1890. The headmaster's house viewed from Albert Park. At this date the Revd W.H. Cam (headmaster 1883-1893) would have been in residence. He came to Abingdon after teaching at Wellington College and following a spell as headmaster of Dudley Grammar School. His time at the school was notable for starting the school magazine, The Abingdonian, in 1890 and re-establishing the Old Abingdonian Club in 1893, although the club had actually been founded in 1743. By 1893 the school roll had fallen to thirty-four: Cam resigned the headship to become Rector of Birchanger in Essex.

Abingdon School, 1890. The new building was opened in 1870 and designed by the local architect Edwin Dolby who lived and worked from his premises in Park Crescent. On the left facing Park Crescent is the headmaster's house. He was also housemaster of school house. In the centre is the Big School with Tower Steps at one end and the bell tower at the other. Under the schoolroom is a large, enclosed, subterranean playground. To the right of the bell tower and entrance hall is the small extension of 1880 comprising three classrooms, the Bennett Room on the top floor also serving as the school chapel until 1901.

West St Helen Street, *c.* 1900. Masters, boys and parents return to Abingdon School following the Founder's Day service in St Helen's church. The schoolboys and their visitors are all splendidly turned out, some ladies towards the rear have raised parasols to keep off the sun. By

contrast, the young girl on the left grasps her doll: the wheelbarrow in the gutter may have been in use to carry horse manure from the street.

Jubilee Celebration, 1897. Abingdon School masters travel in a pony trap while the boys on garlanded bicycles and wearing cerise and white blazers lead the throng up West St Helen Street. On cycles, left to right from front are: H.S. Baker, S.W. Brown, S. Greenwood, F.I.F.

Shepherd, E.E. Insley, V.E. Cook, A.P. Ward, J.E. Montgomery, H.A. Taylor, W.J. Eagle, C.A.W. Payne, S. Trafford, W.B. Collingwood, L.F. Gale and H.E. Johnson at the rear. The young man with an arm in a sling walking on the right-hand pavement is R.N. Turnbull.

Statue of Prince Albert, 1890. The statue by John Gibbs of Oxford was erected in 1864 and is forty-eight feet high. A column stands on a limestone and sandstone pedestal: the whole is surmounted by Prince Albert and shows emblems of parts of the United Kingdom, Borough of Abingdon and Christ's Hospital and dominates the highest part of Albert Park. John Gibbs was well known as the architect of Banbury Cross built in 1859.

Abingdon School, 1952. The school buildings straddle the three playing fields, but now with the additions of classrooms, chapel and gymnasium (1901) designed by Abingdon architect A.B. West; the Science Laboratories (1951) are to the right of the chapel with the Lacies Court property still in private ownership. Shortly to be the fourth playing field, the War Memorial Field beyond Faringdon Road is in agricultural production.

Aerial view of north-west Abingdon, c. 1954. Ock Street prior to building Stratton Way, Bath Street and Albert Park are clearly visible in the foreground. The line of Faringdon Road extends to Shippon and Larkmead School while the land in the Larkhill direction is open and as yet quite undeveloped. This is a remarkably uncluttered view and attests to the relatively slow development of Abingdon in the ninety years between the Albert Park project of the 1860s and the mid-1950s, particularly in this north-westerly direction.

School House, Tower Steps and Big School, c. 1890. This is the western end of Abingdon School, a photograph taken from the headmaster's garden.

Abingdon School, c. 1890. The 1870 building with addition of the 1880 wing housing three extra classrooms.

Abingdon School, *c.* 1900. At the Park Road entrance to the school grounds the Lodge was built in the 1880s as a sanatorium. It has seen service as a small boarding house and is now the Bursary.

St Helen's School, *c.* 1906. The front of the new buildings in Faringdon Road. Like so many village roads at the time, this former turnpike road, then beyond the edge of Abingdon's development, has not been upgraded by Berkshire County Council who took responsibility for it in 1888.

St Helen's School, *c*. 1906. The rear of the buildings seen over extensive flower beds. St Helen's School dates from 1903 but merged with St Katharine's School, Wantage in 1938. St Katharine's was founded in 1897 by the Wantage Order of St Mary the Virgin and the nuns ran the school as part of their teaching wing. The foundation stone of the new building for St Helen's School was laid on 26 May 1904 by the daughter of Queen Victoria, HRH Princess Christian of Schleswig-Holstein, and opened on this site in 1905, having occupied other dwellings in Abingdon until then.

St Helen's School chapel, *c*. 1957. The chapel was built in 1922 to the design of Frank Pearson, who had also designed the main building. Frank Pearson was the son of J.L. Pearson the famous Victorian church architect. The bricks for the building were made in Drayton brickyard.

The Visit of H.R.H. the Princess Christian to Abingdon, and the Ceremony of the - Laying of the Foundation Stone of - ST. HELEN'S SCHOOL, ABINGDON, by - - H.R.H. The Princess Christian,

On THURSDAY, MAY 26TH, 1904.

Programme of the Proceedings.

1.30 p.m.	The 3rd Batt. of the Royal Berks Regiment will arrive from Churn Camp at Abingdon Station and march to the School Site, (via Stert Street, High Street, Ock Street, Spring Road, and Faringdon Road,) where they will form a Guard of Honour and keep the ground.
2.45 p.m.	The Wantage Troop of the Royal Berks Imperial Yeomanry will arrive at the Railway Station to act as an escort to H.R.H. during her visit to Abingdon.
3 p.m.	A Guard of Honour will be formed at the Railway Station by the Abingdon Company of the 1st Vol. Batt. of the Royal Berks Regiment.
3.10 p.m.	H.R.H. the Princess Christian, accompanied by H.H. the Princess Victoria, and attended by Mrs. W. H. Dick-Conyngham, and Major Evan Martin, will arrive at Abingdon Station, and will be received by the Lord Lieutenant of the County, and the Mayor and Town Council who will present an Address to H.R.H.
3.30 p.m.	H.R.H. will proceed to the site of S. Helen's School, via Stert Street, High Street, Ock Street, Conduit Road, Park Crescent, and Faringdon Road.
3.40 p.m.	H.R.H. will arrive at the School site, being received by the Lord Bishop of Oxford, the Founders of the School, and the Committee, who will ask her to lay the Foundation Stone.
4.10 p.m.	A short service of Benediction will then follow at which the Right Rev. the Lord Bishop of the Diocese will officiate and deliver a short address. In the course of this service the Stone will be laid by H.R.H.
4 40 p.m.	H.R.H. will return through the Town to the Abbey, escorted as before, travelling via Spring Road, Park Road, Bath Street, and High Street.

The Clergy of the Parish alone will wear Surplices.

It is particularly requested that none of the Visitors should leave their places until H.R.H. has entered her carriage and left the ground.

Laying the Foundation Stone at St Helen's School, 1904. A copy of the programme itemised the progress of the Royal visit. Princess Helena Augusta Victoria was the daughter of Queen Victoria: she was known as Princess Christian of Schleswig-Holstein following her marriage to Prince Christian in 1866. She was accompanied by her thirty-four year old daughter Princess Victoria. It is interesting to note from the itinerary that the Royal party passed round Albert Park and close to the 1864 statue to Princess Christian's father.

43

The Hooke family, 1912. This family group was taken at the rear of Parkfield in Park Crescent. It shows Mr and Mrs W.H. Hooke together with Emma Hooke, who was Mr Hooke's mother, and nine of their eleven children. Back row, left to right: Margery Annie (1894-1982), William Norman (1895-1966), Kathleen May (1897-1979), Henry Wright (1899-1982), Elizabeth Winifred (1902-1985), Mrs Annie Hooke (1869-1953), Mrs Emma Lording Hooke, Mr W.H. Hooke (1864-1937), Elsie Theodora (1898-1978), Ruth Frances (1908), John Holden Hooke (1907-1988), Violet Christina (1906-1982). Mr and Mrs Hooke moved from Guildford to Abingdon where he was proprietor of the Abbey Press in Stert Street. His youngest son, John Holden Hooke took over the business in 1937 and ran it until his retirement. He was Master of Christ's Hospital and Vice-chairman of Abingdon School, where the Hooke Library is named after him.

Four
Abingdonians

Jubilee celebrations, 1897. The procession is moving along Ock Street to the Square. The banner is of the Bowyer Union Lodges of Oddfellows 3039 and 3228. Other organisations included the Berkshire Order of Foresters, the Provident Institution and the Hearts of Oak.

Jubilee celebrations, 1897. The elder girls followed by the elder boys of the town's elementary schools head this part of the procession. In the Market Place the mayor distributed among them 250 books containing the story of the Queen's life. All children attending the elementary schools received a new penny and a new shilling went to sick children who were unable to attend.

Jubilee celebrations, 1897. Three of the business floats pass along Ock Street. First prize was awarded to J. Gibbens the saddler and harness maker of Broad Street, second prize went to Baylis & Co., printer, on whose float was a model working printing press. Employees distributed copies of the National Anthem which they had printed as the procession passed round the town. Their printing works was in Stert Street with a shop in Market Place. The firm, having been established in 1827, became Burgess and Son about 1907. Third prize went to Morland & Co. (see page 82)

Jubilee celebrations, 1897. The final floats enter the Square from Ock Street. The business procession was preceded by the band of the 1st Volunteer Batt. Queen's Royal West Surrey Regiment. Elsewhere in the parade came Abingdon Oddfellows Brass Band, Abingdon Church Drum and Fife Band, the Wesleyan Drum and Fife band, the Fire Brigade and about thirty decorated floats.

Jubilee celebrations, 1897. In the afternoon, 'water sports took place on Wilsham Reach'. They consisted of 'scratch fours, canoe races, water tournaments, swimming races, water polo &c., lasting until after 6 o'clock'. Land sports then began on the riverside cricket field (Hales Meadow) consisting of races for men, boys and girls, and cycle races, including a 'race for working men riding machines in daily use and ridden in working clothes'.

Jubilee celebrations, 1897. This is part of the regatta on Wilsham Reach and two coxed fours race to the finish line. Later in the evening there was a procession of illuminated boats. 'The boat entered by Roysse's School was an easy winner of the first prize for decorations, the second and third prizes being awarded to the Boys' Church Club and to Mr J.W. Coxeter respectively'. A fireworks display 'made a suitable conclusion to a most enjoyable day'.

Abingdon School Regatta, c. 1900. This appears to be the start of the course near Culham Bridge with stake boats in the centre of the stream and various parents, friends and schoolboys on the river bank. The finish of the course is at the boathouse on Wilsham Reach near the town centre. The wooden footbridge in the background spans Swift Ditch: Culham Bridge is behind. The School Boat Club was flourishing as early as 1840 when it boated from Nuneham, then Wilsham Road and latterly from Culham Reach. Abingdon Rowing Club was formed in 1866.

Abingdon School Regatta, *c.* 1900. The first school regatta was held in July 1892 which was a mixed affair of boys, staff, coaches and Old Abingdonians racing in sculls, pairs and fours. This view looks from Wilsham Road across Andersey Island to the line of trees which shelter the causeway taking the road from Abingdon to Culham Bridge.

Abingdon School Association Football team, 1889-90. Back row, left to right: H.G. D'Almaine, N.A. Saunders, W.L. Russum, F.J.S. Baker, F. Bennetts, F.H. Pryce, R.G. Brown, A.H. Lewis, H.E. Malam, H.L. Driver, T. Hodgson. H.G. D'Almaine was the son of Henry D'Almaine, manager of the London & County Bank in the Market Place: he was appointed Abingdon Borough Treasurer in 1887.

Abingdon School Association Football team, 1907-8. Back row, left to right: W. Leach, O.B. Challenor, K.G. Stevens, F.E. Parker, E.V. Dyke, J.H. Bridgewater, W. Read, W.R. Mortleman, E.H. Harvey, L.W. Holland, L.G. Drewe, W. Edgington, R.B. Leach. There are a number of Abingdon families represented: after the 1927 season the school played Rugby Football.

Athletics, 1901. Abingdon School v Old Boys, Standing, left to right: P. Aldwinckle, A.O.C. Pryce, R.F. Challenor, A.M. Austin, H. Hughes, W.E. Jarman, R.W. Sells, T.F. Bowman, J.R. Hewer, R.N. Turnbill, G.B. Good, G.S. Saxby. Sitting: A.W. Stevens, F.J.S. Baker, F.O. Townsend, C.A.W. Payne, G. Brown, P.L. Deacon, B. Challenor, W. Cottrell, W.T. Morland.

The Public School Sports, 1909. Held at Stamford Bridge on May Day, the Abingdon School team excelled itself winning, jointly with Oundle School, the challenge cup at the centre of the table. Left to right: O.B. Challenor (2nd in quarter mile and 2nd in mile), L.W. Holland (1st three-quarter mile steeplechase, 3rd in mile), G.H.G. Shepherd (1st in hundred yards).

Bury Street School, c. 1914. A fine group of twenty-five pupils in best suits, starched collars and ties with their schoolmaster. Taken in the playground, this photograph may be of the fourteen-year-old leavers.

Bury Street School, *c*. 1910. A small class of boys with their teacher sitting in a classroom divided by a wood and glass partition. Ink wells are full, knib pens at the ready and copy books are open, this must be a writing class.

Bury Street School, *c*. 1927. The whole group looks justly proud for they have just won the Hungerford Banner (displayed) at the Berks, Bucks & Oxon Musical Festival. Back row, left to right: Miss K. Cast, Revd R.C. MacKeown (vicar of Abingdon), A. Bramley, J. Bowen, A. Beer, S. Thomas. Third row: ? Wheeler, ? Pratley, ? Castle, J. Taylor, R. Emerton, ? Heredge, Mr Cambell, Mr R. Spiller (headmaster). Second row: F. Purbrick, T. Branson, C. Humphries, S. Waite, ? Stopps, D. Tubb, G. Denton, R. Turner. Front row: J. Smart, H. King, L. Joyce, B. Allen, J. Simpson, R. Short, E. Cork, H. Jeffries.

Bury Street School, *c.* 1927. Like the boys this group of girls, all twenty dressed in their Sunday best, have been competing at the Berks, Bucks & Oxon Musical Festival and display their Hungerford Banner. The two teachers in the front row hold certificates won at the competition.

Bury Street School, 1911. This small class of twenty-one youngsters seem to be wearing a variety of outer wear, some jackets and shirts having quite elegant collars.

Council School, *c.* 1930. A small class of twenty-four girls with their schoolmistress standing in the far corner of the room. The entrance to the school was by way of Mayott's Road from Ock Street.

Y.M.C.A. Football team, 1914. This group was photographed at the rear of a house which stood in West St Helen Street on the site of the Southern Electric store. Those who can be named are: back row, left to right: -?-, Holdsworth, Argyll -?-. Third row: -?-, Chivers, -?-, -?-, Ted Jarvis, -?-. Second row: -?-, Dacey, H. Pocock, Short, Thouless. Front row: Leach, G. Simpson.

Abingdon Imperial League Football team, *c.* 1930. Back row, left to right: A.W.J. Cross, F.B. Rowlinson, -?-, A.E. Wiggins, H.W.D. Charleton, S.G. Jordon, A.W. Staniland. Second row: R.W. Snell, G.W. Wilks, J.W. Naylor, J.H. Leach, S.C. Marlow, W.J. Smith. Front row: P.S. Chivers, C. Ellis, T.A. Wiggins.

Bury Street School, *c.* 1927. Forty-nine boys, two instructors and two school masters prepare for a swimming lesson in the River Thames at the swimming place near Lock Island: the weir can just be seen behind the group. This public bathing place was opened in 1880: in 1896 a public camping ground was also provided on Lock Island by the Conservators of the River Thames.

Abingdon School Cricket team, 1897. Back row, left to right: J.E. Montgomery, P.L. Deacon, H.E. Johnson, H.E. Taylor, H.A. Shepherd, H.S. Baker, A.J.T. McCreery, E.E. Insley, S.W. Brown, J.S.C. Greenwood, A.P. Ward.

Abingdon School Athletics team, 1935. Back row, left to right: L.P. Mosdell, W.B. Badcock, A.L. Fleet, P.J. Hill, G.E. Sinclair, H.B. Healy, M.R.T. Cooper, M. Thomas, O.E. Clarke, G.A.R. Boyd, D.G. Brown, S.A. Paige, A.R.M. Adams, W.H.G. Mayhead, M.H. Holme, D.R.H. Brown, L.E.J. Luker. L.P. Mosdell became a judge; Sir George Sinclair was deputy governor of Cyprus 1955-60 and Member of Parliament for Dorking 1964-79; Stanley Paige was Master of the Worshipful Company of Carmen 1973-74 and a City businessman.

Abingdon School Cricket, 1950. Standing, left to right: P.R. Sale, D. Free, M. Bateman, P.M. Glassbrook, J.W.R. Ireland, D.W.H. Ridout, M. Glassbrook, P.R. Lucas, J. Furby, I.M. Pickford, T.O. Inwood, B.A. Whiteford.

Abingdon Boxing Club, c. 1939. This group photograph with all the trophies was taken in the old clothing factory which was near St Helen's church and between West St Helen Street and the Brewery. Back row, left to right: -?-, G. Hall, Reg Belcher, Sid Thomas, Ralph Tubb, V. Dorimmey, J. Simpson, Alan Drewitt, Chick Chalkey, Tick Hounslow, Bill Hudson, Jimmy Drew, Geoff Belcher.

M.G. Works fire brigade, 1968. Back row, left to right: A. Purbrick, C. Cox, G. Keen, H. Springfield, B. Saunders, B. Reeve, V. Downes. Front row: E. Stone, J. Simpson, L. Matthews, W. Purbrick.

Home Guard, *c.* 1941. On the visit to inspect the men of local home guards, King George VI is speaking to Sgt R.E. Eason, sometime sub-warden of Radley College and Vice-chairman of Abingdon School governors. Dick Eason came from a Long Wittenham family.

Abingdon School, 1956. The Royal Naval Section of the school CCF being inspected on upper field by General Sir John Winterton, accompanied by Lt L.C.J. Griffin and the headmaster.

Abingdon School, 1957. The Naval inspecting officer is reviewing the brass band and talking to cadet Martin Chambers. Standing, left to right: Lt Hugh Sawbridge (director of music), Major S.C. Parker (contingent commander), James Cobban (headmaster).

Abingdon School, 1956. Founder's Day was the grand event of the school year held at the end of the Summer term to celebrate the refoundation of the school in 1563 by John Roysse. Left to right: Mrs Clifton-Brown, Mrs Lorna Cobban, Mrs Stow, James Cobban (headmaster), Vice-Admiral F. Clifton-Brown (chairman of governors). This was the garden party for parents, Old Boys and friends of the school on Upper Field, which always followed Prize Giving and the Founder's Day Service in St Helen's church.

Abingdon School, 14 June 1963.
HRH Princess Margaret is greeted by
James Cobban at School House.
Mr C.G. Stow (chairman of
governors and managing director
Morland & Co.) is on the right. The
Lord Lieutenant of Berkshire stands
behind Princess Margaret. The Royal
visit was on the occasion of the
Quatercentenary of the re-
foundation of the school, in 1563,
by John Roysse.

Abingdon School, 14 June 1963.
Princess Margaret meets the prefects.
From the left: James Cobban, Nick
Loukes, Roger Burridge, Richard
Ormerod, Keith Dixon, Robin
Moorshead, Michael Ford, Jonathan
Mackenzie, Andrew Foster, Peter
Mann.

St Helen's School, 1914. The complete school outside the new building of 1904. In total there appear to be 101 pupils present: seated in the front row are three young boys! The distinctive porchway and entrance is at the centre of Frank Pearson's 1904 building. The statue of St Helen in a niche above the doorway is similar in style and in detail to the statue of St Helen above the west doorway of St Helen's church.

Abingdon traditional Morris Dancers, 1957. Back row: Jack Hyde, Brian Clarke, Frank Jordan, Ernie Constance, Leslie Argyle. Front row: John Grimsdale, Charlie Brett, Major Francis Fryer, Tom Hemmings (mayor of Ock Street), Stuart Jackson, Leonard Bardwell. Seated: Jim Mooring.

Five

Christ's Hospital, Church, Abbey and Manor

Christ's Hospital, *c.* 1900. Long Alley almshouse in St Helen's churchyard with several almsmen standing outside the porch. The whole building was erected in 1446, the porch added in 1605 and the lantern in 1707. The Masters and Governors of Christ's Hospital meet in the room under the lantern: the former Guild of the Holy Cross pre-dated Christ's Hospital and met in the upper room above the old north porch to St Helen's church.

A Christ's Hospital Almswoman, 1939. She is toasting her bread on the kitchen range with her family pictures and mementos around her. This photograph is one of a series of the almshouses prepared by *The Times*. Christ's Hospital possesses an album presented by *The Times* newspaper.

Christ's Hospital, 1946. The Master, matron and governors of Christ's Hospital, Abingdon, together with the Almsmen and Almswomen; a photograph taken on the lawn at the rear of Long Alley Almshouses.

Governors of Christ's Hospital, 1946. Standing, left to right: H. Carter (Reader), A.E. Tombs, A.C. Longland, O.B. Saxby, R.W. Langford, J.L. Etty, W.M. Coxeter, A.M. Wilson-Green. Seated: W.H. Tombs, A.B. West, T. Bowen (Master), W.T. Morland (Clerk), F. Stimpson (Mayor).

St Helen's church, c. 1960. All is quiet in this late afternoon view of part of East St Helen Street. Here the street narrows down to frame the tower and spire of the church. This is the town church with special pews erected facing the high altar for the mayor and corporation. St Nicolas' church (page 67) in the Market Place traditionally served those who had found employment with the Abbey up to its dissolution in 1538. East St Helen Street was once know as Fore Street: at the same time West St Helen Street was called Back Street.

St Helen's church, 1890. Above the old north porch is the room of the Guild of the Holy Cross, the ancient merchant and charitable organisation. Developing into Christ's Hospital, it transferred its meeting to the Governors' room in the centre of Long Alley almshouses. The Exchequer room above the porch is still owned by Christ's Hospital.

St Helen's church, 1890. The east end of the north aisle showing the font carved in white marble by H.P. Peyman of Abingdon: it is a copy of the Norman font in Sutton Courtenay church and was exhibited at the 1851 Great Exhibition. On the right is the table-top tomb of John Roysse, mercer of London, who re-founded Abingdon School in 1563. He is buried under a stone slab taken from his city of London home in Birchin Lane.

St Helen's church, 1890. The entrance to the outer south aisle from Brick Alley almshouse across the churchyard. The south aisle (1539) is perpendicular in style and ends at the east in a vestry and treasury. The church itself is unusual in having five aisles making its dimensions broader from north to south than it is long.

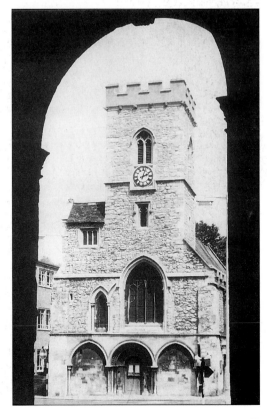

St Nicolas' church, c. 1950. The church, seen from under the County Hall, faces the market Place. It is partly Norman and was badly damaged in 1327 when the townspeople attacked the Abbey and in 1951 when fire gutted the chancel.

Greeting the Bishop of Reading, early Spring 1961. The Bishop of Reading (the Rt Revd Eric Knell) came to Abingdon by boat and was received at St Helen's Wharf close to St Helen's church. Front row, left to right: -?-, E.R. Bailey (churchwarden), Bishop of Reading, D.G. Burrett (mayor), Revd John H.S. Dixon (vicar of Abingdon), Mrs Burrett, John Hooke (churchwarden and proprietor of the Abbey Press), James Cobban (Headmaster Abingdon School).

The Convent of the Order of the Sisters of Mercy, Oxford Road, *c. 1930*. The Order was founded in Dublin in 1831 by Catherine McAuley. In 1860 the first priest of the Abingdon Catholic Mission invited the sisters to Abingdon and they took over a cottage called 'Joy Mount' in Northcourt. Under Mother Elizabeth Rigby the convent moved in 1862 to this site taking over two houses facing Oxford Road and the workhouse. Sir George Bowyer of Radley gave the convent more land to build schools: their boarding school for girls was followed by a boys' school in 1864. At the western end of the original convent lies the chapel built in 1884.

St Edmund's church, 1890. Radley Road is the track across the field in what is a unique scene of rural quiet entirely in contrast to today's heavy traffic and development in this part of the town. Portions of the Workhouse can be seen between the church and presbytery.

St Edmund's church, 1890. The fenced off island of trees between the church and Vineyard Farm House at the junction of Radley and Oxford Roads has long since disappeared and the road been realigned: apart from this, the scene is remarkably unchanged, although the churchyard, which contains a memorial to the 7th Earl of Abingdon designed by Eric Gill in 1928, lost its metal railings to further the war effort. The church is grouped with a gothic presbytery and schoolroom, the latter building faced on to the Oxford Road, and was known as St Edmund's School.

St Edmund's church, 1890. Designed by George Goldie the church was opened in 1857 and is named after Edmund Rich, one of Abingdon's most famous sons who was born in the town in c. 1170. He was appointed Archbishop of Canterbury by the Pope in 1233 and has been canonised as St Edmund of Abingdon.

Our Lady's Convent Junior School, 1949. Front row, fifth and sixth from left: Peter Gray, Peter Benson. Second row, fourth from left: William Dockar-Drysdale, thirteenth and fourteenth: Richard Spring, Ian Fitzsimmons. Third row back, eighth and tenth from left: David Bragg and Patrick Gale. Back row, left: Nigel Hammond.

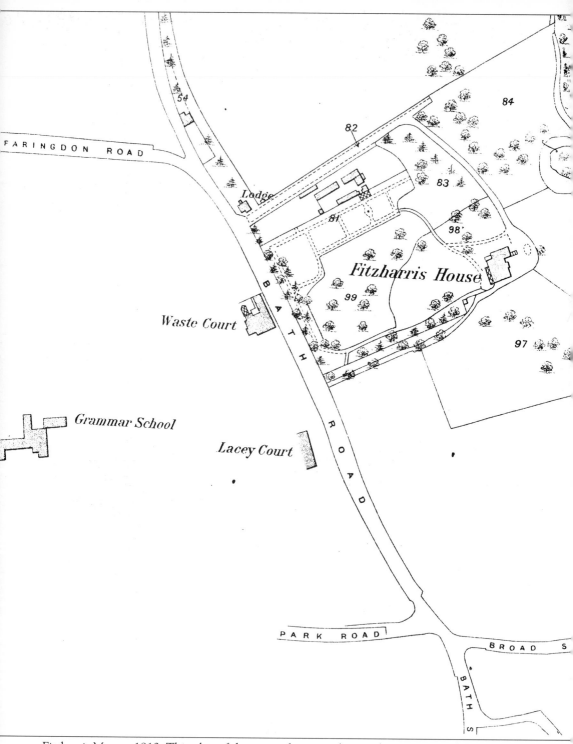

Fitzharris Manor, 1912. This plan of the manor house and grounds accompanied the sale details for the information of intending bidders at the auction, but also shows an interesting contemporary plan of the grounds, parts of which can still be traced in the area.

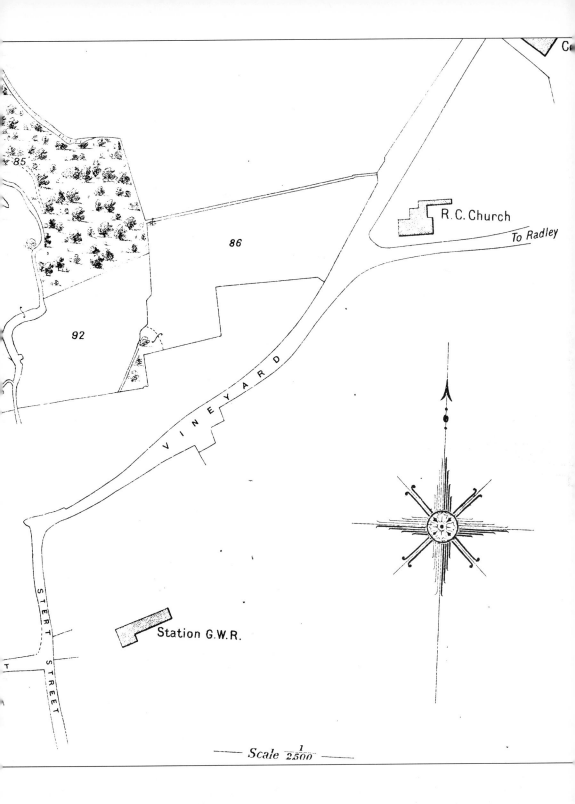

85

86

92

R.C.Church

To Radley

V I N E Y A R D

S
T
E
R
T

S T R E E T

T

Station G.W.R.

Scale $\frac{1}{2500}$

73

ABINGDON-ON-THAMES.

PARTICULARS AND CONDITIONS OF SALE OF A

Highly Attractive

RESIDENTIAL ESTATE

Situate on the outskirts of this Ancient and Historic Borough, one of the favourite resorts of the Upper Thames, known as

"FITZHARRIS,"

COMPRISING A COMMODIOUS

Sixteenth Century Residence

PLACED IN

OLD-WORLD GROUNDS OF EXCEPTIONAL BEAUTY, FINELY WOODED WITH GRAND WELLINGTONIAS, CONIFERÆ AND FOREST TREES, ENTRANCE LODGE AND GARDENER'S COTTAGE, STABLING, GARAGE AND SMALL FARMERY,

TOGETHER WITH

LUXURIANT PADDOCKS,

The whole having an area of nearly

80 ACRES

To be offered for SALE BY AUCTION by

KING, ADKIN & BOWEN

At the "LION" HOTEL, ABINGDON,

On *MONDAY, JUNE 10th, 1912,*

AT 3 FOR 4 O'CLOCK PRECISELY,

By order of the Trustees of the Will of the late J. HEBER CLARKE, Esq.,

IN ONE OR TWO LOTS,

With possession of the whole at Michaelmas next, or of the Residential Portion earlier by arrangement.

Particulars and Conditions of Sale with Plan may be obtained of Messrs. BELCHER, ADKIN & BELCHER, *Auctioneers, Wantage ; of* Messrs. KING, ADKIN & BOWEN, *Auctioneers and Valuers, Abingdon ; and of*

Messrs. NEWMAN, PAYNTER, GOULD & NEWMAN,
1, Clement's Inn, London, W.C.

WILLIAM H. HOOKE, PRINTER, MARKET PLACE, ABINGDON, BERKS.

Fitzharris Manor, 1912. The auction notice for the manor estate following the death of Mr J. Heber Clarke. A number of the trees referred to still grace the site.

Fitzharris Manor, c. 1947. The ancient manor house is shortly to be demolished. A housing estate for scientists at A.E.R.E. Harwell was built in the grounds and began occupancy in late 1947 while a council estate was built over the farmland to the north.

Fitzharris Manor, 1949. Seven eleven-year olds photographed on the steps of the house shortly before its demolition. Sitting, left to right: Tony Gardner, Brian Winkett. Standing Barry Gardner, Gil Pontecorvo, Nigel Hammond, Jonathan Fry, Brian Jenkins. Gil Pontecorvo now lives in Moscow, whither he went with his family in the summer of 1950, when his father, a nuclear scientist at A.E.R.E. Harwell, defected to the Soviet Union. Klaus Fuchs, another notorious atom spy, lived for a while in Lacies Court on the opposite side of Bath Street.

Abbey Gate, 1890. A view from inside the Abbey precinct with St Nicolas' church on the right and former Borough police station on the left. Abbey Gate is now closed to traffic and a new road exits from Abbey Close to the Vineyard at the eastern end of St Nicolas' church.

Abbey House, 1890. A private residence in the ownership of Edwin James Trendell during the third quarter of the last century. He was a prosperous grocer and prominent townsman. The house became the residence of the Bishop of Reading but is now part of the District Council offices.

Abbey Close, *c.* 1950. Within the precinct of Abingdon Abbey this street occupied the border between base court and little court of the monastery.

Lacies Court, 1947. At this time a small hotel under the care of Mrs E.M. Alexander and described as a 'charming manor house, secluded, but near river, bus routes and railway station'. The tariff was £5 5s 0d a week or weekends at a guinea a day. Special terms were available for permanent residents, one of whom for a while was Klaus Fuchs the atom spy. Lacies Court is now the house for the headmaster of Abingdon School and has been incorporated into the school grounds, together with a series of distinctively designed gardens, one known as the Jekyll garden.

Abingdon Abbey, c. 1890. An early photograph taken inside the chequer or Abbey counting house. The giant fireplace leads up to the fine hooded chimney with three lancet-headed piercings for the smoke.

Abingdon Abbey, c. 1950. The Abbey counting house, the chequer, with a unique twelfth-century chimney. Underneath is the Abbot's wine cellar.

Mr Trendell's Folly, *c.* 1950. Edwin James Trendell was 'wholesale and retail grocer, tea dealer, tallow chandler, wine and brandy merchant' with premises in High Street. He built this folly in ecclesiastical style in the garden of his home, Abbey House, which was located within the Abbey precinct.

Cosener's House, 1890. Seen across the river this building is near the site of the Abbey Kitchener's house. He looked after the culinary interests of the monks. After dissolution of the Abbey part of this site came into the hands of the Blacknall family. In recent years the house has been an A.E.R.E. hostel.

Abingdon Borough Regalia. The pair of silver goblets at the rear are hallmarked London 1639 and were presented by Lionel Bostock, woollen draper, Mayor of Abingdon and Master of Christ's Hospital. The Great Mace is silver gilt of 1660 or earlier and very similar in size and pattern to the mace of the House of Commons. Three miniature maces from left to right, date from the reigns of Elizabeth I, Charles I and James II. The mayor's gold chain and badge (1879) is on the left and was presented by John Creemer Clarke, former mayor and last Member of Parliament for the Borough: he was a wholesale clothier and lived at Waste Court in Bath Street. The mayoress' badge was presented by the mayor and past mayors in 1935 to commemorate the Silver Jubilee of George V and Queen Mary.

Six
Morland & Co.

Morland & Co. John Morland started brewing at West Ilsley in 1711. Edward Morland inherited the concern in 1855, bought the Eagle Brewery, Abingdon (1861) then took over Abbey Brewery, Abingdon (1866) forming United Breweries, Abingdon, commemorated in frosted-glass in the windows of the Punchbowl behind County Hall. In the extensive Morland family two became artists, Henry Robert Morland (1716-1797) and George Morland (1763-1804), a connection commemorated in the company logo.

Queen Victoria's Jubilee, 1897. Morland & Co. won third prize in the procession for the best decorated trade car. They exhibited a team of horses and waggons as used in 1837 (Victoria's accession) with another as used in 1897. This is the 1837 waggon in front of Ock Lea, with draymen dressed in 1837 costume.

Brewery staff, *c.* 1914. Each man bears the tool of his particular trade; malt shovel, barley fork, sampling cylinder, measuring stick and soda-water syphon are some of the obvious items. The only men with their hands thrust into their pockets are supervisory; one in the centre wears a bowler hat with his assistant to the right wearing a cap, moustache and gold-watch chain.

Morland staff, *c*. 1900. The entire staff from directors to apprentices seen together in the brewery yard.

Malthouse staff, *c*. 1900. Each man holds the tool of his task in the malthouse: a variety of shovels and forks made from wood.

Queen Victoria's Jubilee, 1897. 'God Save the Queen' says the board in front of this group. All nineteen men wear medals, most a buttonhole, some hold Union Jacks. Hardly a man appears to be aged under fifty. Abingdon Borough Council minutes note that 'after parading the town the procession drew up in the Market Place facing the Queen's statue, around which stood a number of Old Soldiers wearing their medals'. This photograph may have been taken at the brewery after the parade, where they came for their bread and cheese and pint of beer: the medals may be from the Crimean War.

Ock Street, c. 1890. The sales staff outside their offices located each side of the narrow brewery entrance from Ock Street. No. 40 has been turned into The Brewery Tap following closure of both the Crown and Mr Warrick's Arms across the street.

Auction notice for Eagle Brewery, 1861. Edward Morland, then brewing at West Ilsley, bought the Eagle Brewery in Ock Street following the bankruptcy of William Belcher: this remains the site of the present business.

Thomas Skurray, 1912. Mr Thomas Skurray (centre) joined Morland in the 1890s. This remarkable man was formative in the development of the company, having studied brewing on the continent, and was an astute businessman. He was one of the early entrepreneurs of the brewing industry and served a term as chairman of the Brewers' Society. His close association with Morland enabled the company to achieve considerable growth in the half-century from 1890. He was chairman of the company from 1923 to 1938, instrumental in building a new maltings in 1908, a soft-drinks factory in 1910 and a replacement tower brewery in 1912. He also oversaw Morland's acquisition of five breweries in the 1920s: Belcher & Habgood of Abingdon, Dymore Brown and Fergusons of Reading, Hewett & Co of Waltham St Lawrence and the Wantage Brewery. Tom Skurray is photographed with Mr Gillet (right) and Deane Skurray (front) at the topping out of the brewhouse in 1912.

Tower Brewery, built 1912. In red brick with lattice windows and topped with skylights, the tower brewhouse makes its own stylish contribution to the architecture of Abingdon.

Rebuilding the brewhouse, 1911. This tower brewery still dominates the Abingdon skyline and was completed in 1912.

Maltings, c. 1960. The maltings built in 1908 today have the four ventilators removed and the building is converted largely to administrative functions. The new bottling plant has been built on the empty site between boiler house and maltings.

Ock Lea and brewhouse, *c*. 1960. A view from the ancient mulberry tree at the rear of Ock Lea to the lattice windows and skylights of the tower brewery.

Ock Lea, *c*. 1960. Now a small part of the administrative wing of the brewery, this old house on the river Ock was the residence of the Morland family from 1861.

The Brewery from the air, *c.* 1965. A new entrance into the yard from Ock Street can be seen with the tower brewery and maltings beyond. The new bottling plant is in use to the right of the maltings. The site is clearly bounded by the river Ock to the south. The extensive car park beyond the maltings and beside West St Helen Street is partly the site of the former clothing factory. The initial advantage of this site was that all water was drawn from a well near Ock Lea for there were excellent water-bearing strata some 700 feet below this part of Abingdon.

William Tubb, mill hand, seen
emptying a sack of barley into a
hopper at the top of the brewhouse
in about 1955.

Brewery Yard, c. 1960. The old
bottle store is on the left with the
tower brewery opposite. The narrow
exit to Ock Street is at the top of
the yard.

Delivery lorries, *c.* 1950. These pre-war lorries were the first generation to replace horse-drawn drays. Staff on the left are W. Brown and J. Dimond.

Brewery staff, *c.* 1955. Left to right: John Lake, Vernon Polley, Jim Dymore-Brown (head brewer), Charles Brooks, Gordon Barnett and Colin Bycroft at a brewery Christmas party.

Seven

Trade and Business

CULLEN'S STORES, STERT STREET, ABINGDON.

Branches: Corner of Edward Street and Spring Road, and West St. Helen Street, Abingdon.

Postal and Telegraphic Address: "Cullen, Abingdon." Telephone No. 19.

Departments:

Tea,
  Coffee,
    Cocoa,
General Grocery
  and
    Provisions,
Colonial Meat,
  Beef,
Mutton, and
Canterbury
  Lamb
(Best Brands only, Fresh
  Supply Daily).

Departments:

China,
  Glass,
Earthenware,
  Enamelled
    and
Hardware
  Goods,
    Brushes,
Brooms,
  etc., etc.

Established to Supply the Town and Neighbourhood with First Quality Goods at Lowest Cash Prices.

Cullen's Store, 1908. Sidney Cullen took over the store from his father, Edwin, and presided over this shop in Stert Street until it closed in the 1950s: it is now demolished.

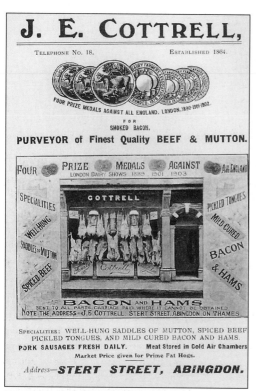

J. E. COTTRELL,

TELEPHONE No. 18.   ESTABLISHED 1864.

FOUR PRIZE MEDALS AGAINST ALL ENGLAND. LONDON.1890-1901-1902.

FOR
SMOKED BACON.

PURVEYOR of Finest Quality BEEF & MUTTON.

FOUR   PRIZE   MEDALS   AGAINST   ALL ENGLAND
LONDON DAIRY SHOWS 1889   1901   1903

SPECIALITIES   COTTRELL   PICKLED TONGUES
    WELL-HUNG   MILD CURED
SADDLES OF MUTTON   BACON
   SPICED BEEF   & HAMS

BACON AND HAMS

SENT TO ALL PARTS CARRIAGE PAID WHERE IT CANNOT BE OBTAINED
NOTE THE ADDRESS - J.E. COTTRELL STERT STREET ABINGDON ON THAMES

SPECIALITIES: WELL-HUNG SADDLES OF MUTTON, SPICED BEEF
PICKLED TONGUES, AND MILD CURED BACON AND HAMS.
PORK SAUSAGES FRESH DAILY.   Meat Stored in Cold Air Chambers
Market Price given for Prime Fat Hogs.

*Address—***STERT STREET, ABINGDON.**

J.E. Cottrell, 1908. Towards the end of the nineteenth century Abingdon had a series of butchers' shops, some adjacent to one or other of the three specialist pig, cattle and sheep markets. Cottrell's in Stert Street is still in business on this site.

Stert Street, Abingdon

Stert Street, c. 1945. Named from the Stert Stream which flowed as an open ditch beside the road: it was covered over from 1791 on a piecemeal basis. At the turn of the century this was one of the town's major shopping streets. The *Abingdon Free Press* of 2 May 1913 reports in detail the great storm at Abingdon. 'The greatest sufferer of all was Mr E. Cullen who has three shops besides store rooms in Stert Street. The cellars were filled with all kinds of dry goods, such as fruit, sugar, soap, soda, all of it was absolutely destroyed. Mr Cullen lost at a rough estimate, over £600.'

Beesley & Son, c. 1884. William Beesley, who had worked for Hannah Harris for over thirty years, was left this business in Hannah's will in 1883: he changed the name from Harris & Tomkins to Beesley & Son. It is probably William Beesley standing on the door step, but he died shortly after Hannah's bequest and the business continued under Mrs Beesley and her three sons. In due course the youngest son took over in 1895 and the shop became known as E.H. Beesley.

E.H. Beesley, c. 1900. Inside the men's department of the shop, selling cases and Gladstone bags, overcoats, trousers, jackets, cotton sheets and waistcoats, the latter priced from 5/6 (27p) to 10/6 (52p) each. Note the gas lamp on the central beam.

E.H. Beesley's staff outing, *c.* 1910. E.H. Beesley is holding the traces on the left: there are some wonderful ladies from the Victorian era sitting inside the coach. The tall young man standing fourth from the left is Oswald Barrett, son of J.P. Barrett of West Hanney, who became apprenticed to E.H. Beesley in 1908. After war service Oswald Barrett returned to Beesley's and became junior partner in 1921; five years later he married E.H. Beesley's eldest daughter, Gladys. On the death of Ernest Herbert Beesley in 1949, Oswald Barrett became senior partner in the firm, running it with his wife and her two younger sisters, Phyllis and Madge Beesley.

Delivery Van, *c.* 1912. This distinctive vehicle provided an eye-catching moving advertisement for E.H. Beesley's High Street store. It was probably the first example in Abingdon of the change from horse transport for such a purpose. Note the klaxon horn and a starting handle between the two wheels.

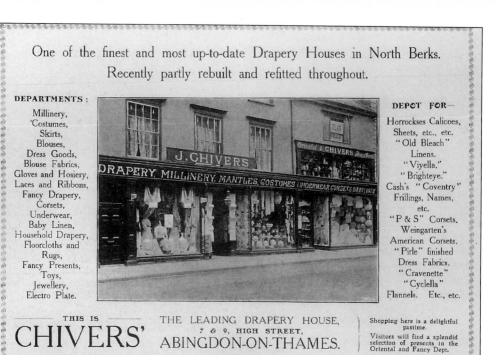

One of the finest and most up-to-date Drapery Houses in North Berks.
Recently partly rebuilt and refitted throughout.

DEPARTMENTS:

Millinery,
Costumes,
Skirts,
Blouses,
Dress Goods,
Blouse Fabrics,
Gloves and Hosiery,
Laces and Ribbons,
Fancy Drapery,
Corsets,
Underwear,
Baby Linen,
Household Drapery,
Floorcloths and
Rugs,
Fancy Presents,
Toys,
Jewellery,
Electro Plate.

DEPOT FOR—

Horrockses Calicoes,
Sheets, etc., etc.
"Old Bleach"
Linens.
"Viyella."
"Brighteye."
Cash's "Coventry"
Frillings, Names,
etc.
"P & S" Corsets.
Weingarten's
American Corsets.
"Pirle" finished
Dress Fabrics.
"Cravenette"
"Cyclella"
Flannels. Etc., etc.

THIS IS
CHIVERS'
THE LEADING DRAPERY HOUSE,
7 & 9, HIGH STREET,
ABINGDON-ON-THAMES.

Shopping here is a delightful pastime.
Visitors will find a splendid selection of presents in the Oriental and Fancy Dept.

Chivers' 1908. An advertisement for this well-known High Street drapery house.

Chivers', c. 1925. This ladieswear and drapery business was acquired by E.H. Beesley in 1926 and was located at 7-9 High Street, occupied by Modern Music today. The Beesley concern sold the business in the late 1940s. The shop frontage advertised its wares as selling drapery, millinery, mantles, costumes, underwear, corsets, baby linen and fancy goods, toys and dolls.

J.N. Paul Ltd, *c.* 1924. Paul's was originally a jewellers shop situated on the site of today's Lloyds Bank on the corner of Ock Street and Winsmore Lane. The business was acquired by E.H. Beesley in 1922 and moved to this site at 16 High Street as a clothing shop.

J.N. Paul Ltd, *c.* 1956. Paul's moved again to 26 High Street with demolition of the previous shop to make way for an early Woolworth store. In this photograph it is next door to Beesley's main shop and selling shoes.

H.J. Brooks, photographer. Henry Brooks was in business in Abingdon in the late 1860s and 1870s: his cards variously describe him as photographer, bookseller and artist. These pictures, found in a family album at a house in St John's Road, clearly illustrate his style of portraiture but are of unknown subjects. Nevertheless, it is likely the man and woman are husband and wife: the third photograph probably shows father and daughter for she bears a facial resemblance to the older woman. The young man with the deerstalker hat (opposite, above) could well be an advertisement for His Master's Voice!

Henry Taunt, (1842-1922) had a distinct photographic interest in Abingdon, the Thames and neighbouring villages by completing over 3,000 compositions of the area during his lifetime in which he is believed to have taken some 53,000 negatives. He wrote and illustrated books concerning the Thames in which Abingdon featured: his *Ancient and Modern Abingdon* was any early history and guide to the town. Henry J. Brooks operated in the town particularly in the 1860s and 1870s, but may have found business best in studio photographs (pages 20, 101-2). Other Abingdon photographers were J.G. Brewerton with a studio in the High Street in the 1890s, W.J. Vasey and Warland Andrew whose photographs of sheep in the Abbey Gateway (page 2, 24) is distinctive. More recent photographers recording the Abingdon scene have been H.J. Milligan and Ivor Fields (page 89).

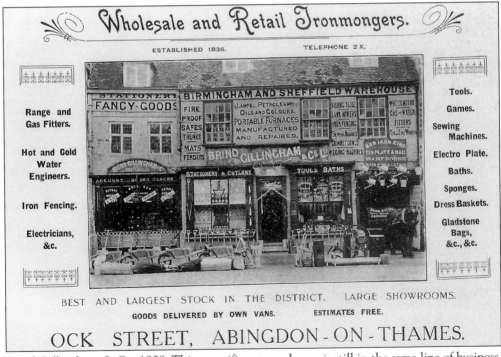

Brind Gillingham & Co, 1908. This magnificent warehouse is still in the same line of business under proprietorship of the Beadle family.

BIRMINGHAM, SHEFFIELD, & LONDON

WAREHOUSE,

OCK STREET, ABINGDON.

CHARLES COXETER,

MANUFACTURER OF

Pattens, Clogs, and Tin Ware.

WHOLESALE AND RETAIL DEALER IN

Dessert, Table, and Carver Knives and Forks, Steels
Pen and Pocket Knives
Razors and Scissors
Snuffers, Corkscrews
Fenders, Fire-irons
Coal Shutes, Bellows
Frying Pans, Saucepans, and Boilers
Enamelled Ware
Candlesticks
Copper, Iron, and Tin Tea Kettles
Superior Metal Tea and Coffee Pots
Spoons—Silver, Electro-Plated, German, Britannia Metal, and Iron
German Silver, and Plated German and Silver Forks, Sugar Tongs, Toast Racks, &c.
Improved Dish Covers
Brass Taps
Flocks, Mops, and French Clogs
Papier Mâché Tea Trays, Inkstands, Card Racks, &c.
Japan Tea Trays, Waiters, Spice Boxes, &c.

Accordions
Work Boxes, Cash Boxes, Desks
Portfolios, Dressing Cases, Tea Caddies
Looking Glasses, &c.
Combs—Tortoiseshell, Horn, and Ivory
Brushes—Hair, Tooth, Nail, Shaving, Cloth, Shoe, &c., &c.
Spectacles, Beads, Purses
Watch Guards, Chains, Keys, Seals
Snaps, Purse Sets
Jewellery, and Wedding Rings
Silver Thimbles, Tooth Picks
Pen and Everpoint Cases
Snuff Boxes, Strops and Hones
Padlocks, French Baskets
Carpet Bags, Travelling Trunks
Fishing Tackle
Cut and Moulded Glass
China Ornaments
Toys in great variety
Fancy and General Stationery, &c.
Perfumery, Sponge, India Rubber
Congreves, &c., &c.

Old Gold, Silver, Rags, Waste Paper, Metals, Horse-Hair, Bones, Skins, and Iron, bought or exchanged.

TERMS—READY MONEY.

Coxeter & Sons, Ock Street. Three advertisements for this major town business. Starting broadly from a rag and bone business Coxeter's expanded. By 1907 the business and extended on both sides of Ock Street. Even in the late 1940s this extensive emporium was a veritable magpie's nest for the country housewife.

COXETER & SONS, LTD.,

Clincher and Dunlop Tyres Stocked.   Michelin Stockists.

Motor and Cycle Experts

Sole District Agents for
HUMBER, ARGYLL, DARRACQ, CLEMENT-TALBOT, ROVER & SWIFT **Cars.**

GARAGE.   PITS.
ACCUMULATORS RE-CHARGED.

Cars for Hire.

Agents for
SWIFT,   SINGER,   ROVER,
HUMBER & RUDGE-WHITWORTH

Bicycles.

Large Stocks of both Motor and Cycle Accessories.

CYCLE REPAIRS.

REPAIRS BY STAFF OF EXPERIENCED ENGINEERS.

32, Ock Street, ABINGDON-ON-THAMES,

Telephone 82Y, Abingdon.
Telegrams: Coxeters, Abingdon.   **and at NEW ROAD GARAGE, OXFORD.**   Telephone, 106Y, Oxford.
Telegrams: Coxeters, Motors, Oxford.

The Square and Ock Street, 1890. A drinking fountain is in the centre of the Square where the War Memorial now stands. Behind the railed-off garden is the Independent Chapel designed by J.S. Dodd and built in 1862. Ock Street had a little traffic of horse-drawn delivery carts and was one of Abingdon's main business streets.

The Rising Sun, 1895. Situated at the junction of Bath Street and the Square (formerly Sheep market and Boar Street), this temperance hotel had a limited lifespan: it is recorded in 1854 but was demolished about 1900, perhaps not surprisingly in a town with upwards of forty-five other hotels, inns and taverns all selling wines, beer and spirits.

Ock Street, c. 1900. Entrance to Morland's brewery is through the gap between the two buildings: the left window advertises Burgoyne's wines and Harvest Burgundy and the door indicates Morland's sales office.

Ock Street, *c.* 1950. The same Morland buildings reworked in Brewers' gothic. In recent times 40 Ock Street, on the right of the brewery entrance, has been converted and opened as the Brewery Tap following closure of the Crown and Mr Warrick's Arms on the opposite side of the street.

Cottrell's Fish and Game shop, *c.* 1914. T.A. Radbourn's shop in Stert Street (see opposite) became part of Cottrell's butchery business: Mr George Maltby wearing the cap stands on the right of the display.

T. A. Radbourn,

Telephone No. 17. Established Half-a-Century.

ℲISHMONGER,

POULTERER & ICE MERCHANT,

Licensed Dealer in :: Game.

COUNTRY ORDERS PUNCTUALLY ATTENDED TO.

FAMILIES WAITED UPON DAILY FOR ORDERS.

23, Stert Street, Abingdon.

T.A. Radbourn, 1908. One of the specialist shops in the meat trade dealing in fish, poultry and game. At the turn of the nineteenth century Abingdon also had three pork butchery shops and a sausage maker.

Floods in Ock Street, 1947. Mr Fred Stimpson gives some of his customers a helping hand from his general store at 149 Ock Street. Mrs Stimpson is standing in the centre of the shop doorway, Mrs Joyce Maltby is on the far left of the group and Mrs Violet Wheeler carries the basket on the right of Mr Stimpson.

Caldecott Walk and the Wilts & Berks Canal, c. 1890. Caldecott House, seen behind the wall, was home to the Hyde family. During this century it was a hotel, then a Dr Barnardo's home. Demolished in 1972 the grounds have been built over for housing. The Wilts & Berks Canal was opened to Abingdon in 1810, closed in 1906 and abandoned by 1914. Its main function was to bring cheaper coal to Abingdon and the Vale of the White Horse from Somerset and the Forest of Dean. In 1838 near the height of its activity 9,930 tons of coal were unloaded at Abingdon wharf, but in 1870 with competition from the railway only 340 tons came to Abingdon. Beyond the open Caldecott lifting bridge the canal broadened into the wharf at the junction with the Thames, around which are the canal company's warehouses.

Ock Street, 1890. Looking east from close to the junction with Conduit Road. The shop on the left is J. Leonard, plumber and decorator. The range of buildings on the right has largely been demolished to make way for Ballards and the Post sorting office. Prominent among them is the Methodist chapel in early gothic design by Wilson of Bath, 1845: two doors beyond is a dairy shop selling milk, butter and cheese.

The Abingdon train, *c.* 1960. The one-coach train, known as the Abingdon bunk, leaves the town for Radley: malthouses behind the Vineyard are in the background. The line was opened on 2 June 1856 by the Abingdon Railway Company as broad gauge track: it was taken over by the Great Western Railway in 1904.

M.G. Car factory, 1980. The half-millionth MGB is ceremonially rolled off the production line. Sid Enver, on the right, is shaking hands with Geoff Iley across the roof of the car. Jim Simpson stands on the right wearing a white coat.

Eight
A View of the Villages

Steventon, c. 1910. Looking south towards Steventon Hill along High Street. The wooden building on the right is the old smithy at the junction of High Street and the Causeway. The village War Memorial is now behind the signpost on the island of grass between the Causeway and Hanney Road.

The Fox Inn, Steventon, *c*. 1930. This inn provided refreshment for travellers and also petrol for their motors from the old-style Shell pumps. Until recent years the Fox stood on the Birmingham to Bournemouth road and had the advantage of equidistance from each town.

Steventon, *c*. 1969. Jack Cox at the North Star on Steventon Causeway pours a pint of Morland bitter. His family has been at the inn since 1842 when great-great-grandfather Cox took over the inn combining work with the blacksmith's shop opposite. The inn came to Morland & Co. with their take-over of Wantage Brewery Co.

Marcham, *c.* 1895. A traction engine made at Wantage Engineering Company's foundry meets a pony trap on Marcham Common. It is likely the driver of the engine is holding the horse while the occupant of the trap tries his hand on the engine.

West Hanney, *c.* 1910. Looking from the church to the thatched blacksmith's shop on the green. The raised and flagged causeway each side of the road attests to the wetness of this 'island' in the Vale of the White Horse: the causeway extends over a mile to East Hanney.

West Hanney, *c.* 1920. Looking east along Church Street to the Plough Inn on the left. Church Farm together with the bakery and grocer's shop lies at the far end of this part of the village green. The upper stage of the church tower was demolished and replaced by a 'temporary' corrugated iron cover until the present stone and slate tower was erected.

East Hanney, *c.* 1909. Looking north towards the malthouse and church. On the left is Sunnyside with overhanging timbers at first floor level, while on the right is the chapel and malthouse in the distance. The road surface and footpaths are unmade and were liable to become very muddy in wet weather.

Sutton Courtenay, *c.* 1910. The Swan inn, village green and All Saints' church. In the churchyard now lie buried Prime Minister Asquith, who retired to the Wharf in the village as Earl of Oxford and Asquith, and E.A. Blair, better known as George Orwell, author of *Animal Farm* and *1984*.

Sunningwell church from the south-east, *c.* 1890. A decade earlier J.P. Seddon had restored the church of St Leonard and designed the glass portraits in the east window. The unique west porch is supposed to have been the gift of Bishop Jewel of Salisbury who was Rector of Sunningwell in the 1550s: it is seven-sided with the entrance from the north.

The Tandem, Kennington, *c.* 1915. This thatched and ornamented tile-hung village inn has a horse-drawn Morland dray delivering supplies: it is a world apart from the inn of the same name which stands on the site today.

Long Wittenham, 1890. The lane into the churchyard passes between barns and the timbered and jettied front of Church Farm: a mud-and-thatch wall links the churchyard to the farmhouse. In the shade of the barn a pony and trap take shelter from the late afternoon sun.

Day's Lock, c. 1910. So called probably after the first lock keeper here. Day's Lock provides excellent views of Wittenham Clumps and the Sinodun Hills. The old lock keeper's house is on the island to the right of the metal footbridge leading to Little Wittenham.

Dyke Hills, 1890. The site is Iron Age and comprises two massive ramparts with a ditch between them. On the other side natural protection of the 114 acre site is offered by the Rivers Thame and Thames. In this view the medial ditch is divided by sheep hurdles with a substantial flock penned at the far end.

Little Wittenham, c. 1910. A lady rests her skiff near Little Wittenham footbridge which takes walkers from Dorchester and Day's Lock into the village. The lock keeper's house upstream of the bridge has been demolished and is replaced by a Thames Conservancy house immediately above the lady's skiff.

Culham Lock, c. 1890. The lock keeper is laboriously opening a sluice to empty one of the deepest locks on the river which has an average fall of seven feet. There is an open view over the lock to Culham village and hurdles have been placed in the foreground to keep grazing sheep back from the lock chamber. The lock is two miles downstream from Abingdon Bridge on Culham Cut, a river channel cut between Culham Reach and Sutton Bridge to improve navigation and avoid difficult water through Sutton Courtenay.

Culham College, the south entrance and drive, 1890. This Church of England Teachers' Training College was founded by Bishop Wilberforce of Oxford in 1852. It now houses the European School.

Culham College, 1890. The building's architect was Joseph Clarke and the complex was originally intended to house ninety-six students.

Culham College, 1890. The college was built round three sides of a square (the fourth side was added in 1930 to form a quadrangle). A cloister was formed by a lean-to building on wooden supporting pillars, all in a severe institutional style.

Culham College, 1890. The chapel (centre) was somewhat lighter in design than the grim Victorian gothic to be found elsewhere in Bishop Wilberforce's complex. A separate schoolroom (right) was formerly used as a local church school and for student teaching practices.

118

Culham Bridge, 1890. Built over Swift Ditch, a backwater of the Thames on the eastern end of Andersey Island, this dry exit from Abingdon was erected in 1416 by the mediaeval Guild of the Holy Cross. The other parts of the dry route included the causeway over Andersey Island and Abingdon Bridge, also built in 1416. An important Civil War skirmish took place on Culham Bridge in January 1645, when Sir Henry Gage, Royalist Governor of Oxford, with 1,800 horse and foot soldiers attacked the bridge. Gage was killed in the encounter and Abingdon remained in Parliamentarian hands.

Culham church, 1890. St Paul's church faces the centre of the village green. The tower was rebuilt in 1710 but Joseph Clarke, architect of Culham College, also rebuilt the remainder of the building in 1852 in thirteenth century style: the chancel was in turn rebuilt some twenty years later in 1872 by R. Phené Spiers.

Clifton Hampden, 1890. The village was described in 1878 as 'nestling in great shade-trees, and the church was of more than ordinary beauty and interest. The Thames winds placidly by, past elms and beeches, and under willows, and every little bay where there is still water is covered with yellow lilies.'

Clifton Hampden, 1890. Unsealed dust lanes meet, that to the right passes over Clifton Hampden Bridge to the Barley Mow and Long Wittenham. Ahead is the church perched on a cliff above the river. The conversation piece on the left is taking place outside the barn near Thames View Cottage.

Clifton Hampden, 1890. A longer view towards the church with scattered thatched cottages and barns on the left. On the other side of the road orchards run down to the river bank. Elm trees shade the road and neat garden hedges form an orderly border to keep at bay the flocks and herds of animals which would have been driven along these lanes to pasture and water.

Clifton Hampden, 1890. Looking from the church towards the junction with the Long Wittenham road past thatched cottages and timber barns. Even elm trees grow into the side of the carriageway, which is not too surprising since what traffic there was would generally be in the middle of the road.

Clifton Hampden Bridge, 1890. Henry Taunt's camera takes a peep through the trees from the west front of the church to Sir George Gilbert Scott's fine bridge over the Thames. The church is high on a cliff above the water and this is one of those places where the river flows rapidly over a hard bed rather than over gravel or silt. A consequence was that goods to and from Abingdon and Oxford were often transhipped at Burcot wharf and taken by road rather than face the shallows in the river between Clifton and Oxford.

Clifton Hampden Bridge, c. 1910. Built to replace a ferry, this bridge was designed by Scott and built with coarse bricks made in the locality. In *Till I End my Song*, Robert Gibbings noted the house martins' nests under the arches. In 1939 he counted 128 of them; by the 1950s there were 400 each year. In 1959 the Nature Conservancy scheduled the bridge a site of scientific interest.

Clifton Hampden, 1890. A close-up view of one of Scott's most successful projects, this gothic style brick bridge. The toll remains on the Berkshire bank: the Barley Mow inn is a few yards beyond.

The Barley Mow Inn, c. 1890. This timber-cruck constructed riverside inn is on the former Berkshire side of Clifton Hampden bridge. Under its thatched roof is one of the oldest inns on the river, which dates from 1350. Jerome K. Jerome features the Barley Mow in *Three Men in a Boat*.

Clifton Hampden, 1890. A panoramic view from across the river. On the right is the spirelet of St Michael's church, set on a low cliff above the river and virtually rebuilt by Sir George Gilbert Scott in 1844 and 1866. In the churchyard a stone cross marks the grave of Sgt William Dykes of the Grenadier Guards who accidentally let-off his rifle and was consequently the first man in Wellington's army to fire a shot at the Battle of Waterloo. The notice board beside the river advertises the Plough inn up in the village, then run by C.F. Wake. Interestingly, each one of the thatched cottages seems to have a modest wooded privy at the top of its garden.

Nuneham Park, 1890. The Mansion is within three miles of Abingdon Market Place and its building was started by Simon, first Lord Harcourt in 1756, who engaged Stiff Leadbitter of Eton as architect. In 1777 the second Lord Harcourt commissioned Launcelot 'Capability' Brown to improve the grounds; he also consulted John Carr of York and Robert Adam concerning alterations to the house.

124

Nuneham Park, 1890. When 'Capability' Brown landscaped the grounds between 1779 and 1782 he formed a series of Thames vistas with 'hanging' woods over the river and winding pathways. William Whitehead had Brown conversing with Nature in his poem *The Late Improvements at Nuneham*, so impressive was Brown's transformation of the park.

Nuneham Park, *c.* 1882. Brown's ornate cottage was always an important focal point for outings both from Abingdon and Oxford on foot, but especially in summer months by the river.

Nuneham Lawn on a fête day, c. 1890. George Granville Harcourt wrote to Abingdon's mayor and corporation in 1861 acknowledging the mayor's letter of thanks to Harcourt for allowing Abingdon's townsfolk to visit the grounds at Nuneham. 'It gives me much pleasure to see my grounds and Park enlivened by the resort of those who think it worth while to come there', he replied.

Nuneham Park, 1890. The riverside walk through the hanging woods of Nuneham culminating in the thatched cottage orné and rustic wooden bridge.

Nuneham Park, 1890. The end of Brown's riverside walk was the rustic bridge leading from Lock Wood to the island downstream from Nuneham and close to the thatched cottage.

Nuneham Park, 1890. The old conduit head was displaced from Carfax in Oxford when High Street was widened in 1787 and it became a nuisance to coaches. It was presented to Lord Harcourt who had it set up in the park as an eye catcher or folly. It was built in 1610 by Otto Nicholson, whose initials are carved on the structure, its original purpose being the supply to the City of Oxford of pure water brought from the hills above North Hinksey. This was an unusual kind of park decoration for the period when it was set up, for then follies and sham gothic castle ruins were all the vogue. Before the presentation a castle had in fact been projected for the site on which the conduit stands.

Acknowledgements

I am grateful to all those local people who offered me photographs of Abingdon and the surrounding villages and to those who suggested interpretations of some of the more mysterious images. This book has been made possible by the generosity of the following:

Abingdon School Archives (Mr Michael St J. Parker),
Abingdon School Library (Mrs A. Soper), St Helen's School (Mrs Galloway),
The Master and Governors of Christ's Hospital (Mr Michael Matthews, Master),
Morland & Co. (Mr Arthur Brown), Mr Ivor Fields, Mr John Saywell,
E.H. Beesley (Abingdon) Ltd (Mr David Barrett), Miss Joy Alexander, Mrs K. Booker,
Mr John Carter, Sir James Cobban, Mrs Joyce Parsons, Mrs Angela Potter, Mrs Rosemary
Pryor, Mr Hugh Randolph, Mr D.J. Seabrook, Mr J.T. Simpson, Mr David Milton
and Mr A. Poulson. The Spring 1996 WEA Local History Course in Abingdon
was an ever-present source of good advice.

Books and publications consulted:
St Nicolas Abingdon & other papers, A.E. Preston (1929, reprinted 1971)
A History of Abingdon, J. Townsend (1910, reprinted 1972)
The Wilts & Berks Canal, L.J. Dalby (1971)
Rural Life in the Vale of the White Horse, 1760-1914 (1974, reprinted 1993) *The White Horse
Country* (1972), *The Book of Abingdon*, Nigel Hammond (1979)
Abingdon in Camera, M.J. Thomas (1979)
Church and School, James Cobban (1963)
Nuneham, Mavis L. Batey (1970)
Abingdon Essays, W.J.H. Liversidge and J.H. Liversidge (1989)
The Abingdon Corporation Plate, A.E. Preston and Agnes C. Baker (1958)
Historic Streets of Abingdon, Agnes C. Baker (1957)
Selections from the Records of the Borough of Abingdon, Bromley Challenor (1898)
A History of Rowing at Abingdon School, 1840-1990, R.G. Mortimer (1990)